Hold My Glitter

Overcoming Obstacles in Ministry

Debbie Rhoads

KIDZMATTER
PUBLISHING

Hold My Glitter: Overcoming Ministry Obstacles

Published by KidzMatter
432 East Val Lane, Marion, IN 46952

kidzmatter.com

Printed in the United States of America

Cover Design by Andrew Brooks,
andrewbrooks.crtv@gmail.com

Book Layout by Nicole Jones, kneecoalgrace@gmail.com

Edited by Kay Williams

ISBN: 979-8-9850095-1-4
ISBN (ebook): 979-8-9850095-2-1

To Julie, Laura, and Hollie

We have overcome some serious obstacles together. Even though God has us doing ministry across three different time zones from each other, I am beyond blessed knowing I can count on you to *Hold My Glitter.*

Table Of Contents

Foreword by Ryan Frank

It is with great joy that I introduce to you *Hold My Glitter: Overcoming Obstacles in Ministry* by Debbie Rhoads. Debbie is not only an amazing children's pastor and esteemed faculty member at KidMin Academy, but she is also a dear friend of our family and a favorite speaker at The KidzMatter Conference. Her profound insights and unwavering faith have inspired countless individuals in the children's ministry community, and this book promises to do the same for you.

In this compelling book, Debbie shares her personal journey of overcoming adversity and transforming challenges into opportunities for growth and faith.

As a children's ministry leader, Debbie's love for glitter is more than a simple preference for sparkle. It represents her unwavering belief in the beauty and potential of every challenge we face. Glitter, in Debbie's world, symbolizes the unique aspects of our lives and ministries that, when entrusted to God and supportive friends, can transform obstacles into opportunities for growth, faith-building, and character development.

Hold My Glitter is not just a book; it is an invitation to embrace a new perspective on the trials and tribulations we encounter in ministry. Debbie encourages us to see beyond the immediate difficulties and recognize the divine lessons and blessings that lie within. Her message is clear: we are not alone in our struggles, and together, with God's guidance and the support of our community, we can overcome even the most daunting challenges.

Debbie's approach is both practical and deeply spiritual. She provides actionable steps and strategies for overcoming obstacles while also reminding us of the importance of prayer, trust, and reliance on God's strength. Her unique blend of practicality and spirituality makes this book an invaluable resource for anyone involved in ministry.

In *Hold My Glitter*, Debbie has given us a gift. She has opened her heart and shared her story, offering us a roadmap to navigate the challenges of ministry with grace, faith, and resilience. Her words are a testament to the power of God's love and the strength we find in community.

Debbie is a beacon of hope and a source of inspiration for all of us in the children's ministry community. Her dedication, wisdom, and faith shine brightly in this book, and I have no doubt that *Hold My Glitter* will be a source of encouragement and empowerment for you, just as it has been for me.

With gratitude and anticipation, I invite you to dive into the pages of this remarkable book. May it strengthen your faith, renew your spirit, and equip you to overcome any obstacle in your path.

Introduction

My parents divorced when I was a young child. My mom had remarried a man who became an alcoholic. It was very rare not to see a beer in the hand of my stepdad. I have vivid memories of him, beer in hand, with a group of his buddies. All being drunk, the group of men would challenge each other to do things none of them had any business doing. Example: "Hey, I bet you can't throw this pocketknife from here and get it to stick in that tree over there." In his drunken stupor, my stepdad would say, "Hold my beer." He would pass off his beer and try to show that he could complete the challenge, most of the time failing.

Out of all the memories of my early child-hood, I am not sure why this one remains.

However, God has taken that memory and helped me visualize something, all while redeeming the phrase, "Hold my beer." God made me to be a visual person, so it is very common for memories and situations to be turned into a lesson for me. I love how God works that way because now I get to share it with you, and I pray it impacts your life the way it has impacted mine.

As a children's ministry leader, one of the things you will commonly find in my hand is glitter. In my opinion, glitter can and should be used on everything. In this visual lesson that God has shown me, the glitter I hold is not just tiny, colorful, sparkly fragments of awesomeness. The glitter represents specific things in my life. When I say, "Hold my glitter," and hand it off to someone as I strive to overcome an obstacle within ministry, who I hand it off to matters. The obstacles that are overcome are more than mere challenges. They are opportunities that strengthen, build faith, and create Godly character. This analogy may seem strange; however, I encourage you to lean into it. I promise that it will make sense.

I assume you picked up this book because you have had moments where obstacles completely overwhelm you. You may be experiencing moments right now. My friend, you are not alone. You can and will overcome. Together, we will tackle some of the most difficult obstacles we face in ministry -- from volunteer shortages to an overwhelming task load, to the obstacle of ourselves. God did not call you into ministry for you to be defeated. So say it with me, "Hold my glitter!" Let's overcome some obstacles.

Don't Tell Me
I Can't Do Something

There is nothing more motivating than when someone says, "You can't do that…" I will prove to you I can, and I will do it with a baby on my hip, puke on my shirt, a toddler around my leg, while teaching fifty first graders about Shadrach, Meshach, and Abednego. Don't tell me I can't do something. Hold my glitter and watch me shine!

Several years ago, I was at a retreat for children's ministry veterans. All of the leaders present had been in children's ministry for ten years or more. It was a weekend dedicated to refresh and renew our spirits so as to carry on the calling that God had put on our lives. If you have been in the ministry for any amount of time, you know that when you get a group of children's ministry leaders together in a room, the topic always finds its way to poop. It's inevitable. This weekend was no exception. We shared heartfelt stories of God working in the lives of the children to whom we minister. We swapped ideas about volunteer appreciation. We shared about the difficult obstacles we have overcome. And then…somehow the topic turned to poop. The funny thing about it is, none of us were surprised.

Our conversation turned into a competition of who had the best poop story from their ministry. I sat quietly, intently listening to each story as everyone laughed, groaned, and even dry-heaved a couple of times. The stories were great, but I knew that I had the best story of all and that I would shut the competition down, so I patiently waited to be the last person to share. I was that confident.

Finally, it was my turn as one of my fellow kidmin friends said, "I don't know, Debbie. Can you top this?" I boldly stood up, intertwined my fingers to give them a good pop, moved my neck side to side to feel the crack, and postured myself to take down the competition as I said, "Hold my glitter!" I then proceeded to tell my infamous poop story. It was fantastic and absolutely disgusting at the same time. You will have to wait until Chapter 6 to read my award-winning story. (Don't be skipping ahead. Trust the process.) By the end, it was clear that I had won the day. My poop story won the award out of all the other poop stories. It was a proud moment.

It is within our human nature to compete. Competition gives us motivation to succeed and to better ourselves; however, competition can activate our survival instinct, and we become obsessed with winning. If not kept in check, we become consumed with besting our peers, being on top, and never allowing losing to be an option…ever, even when we do lose.

Throughout this book, the phrase "Hold My Glitter," will take on dual meanings. The first meaning is the healthy competitive, "Hold My Glitter." It says, "Watch me! I WILL overcome! I WILL tackle that obstacle! It may look like the odds are stacked against me, but I have God on my side. He is fighting the battle with me, so step out of the way while I crush this!"

This kind of Godly confidence is what we want. The confidence knowing that God's got us and nothing stands against us. However, we are human, and sometimes our humanness sneaks in and that Godly confidence turns into cockiness just to prove people wrong. This is a slippery slope. Our confidence turns into defiance, and no matter what you must do or who you have to step on or who it may affect, you will win. May I remind you that our overcoming obstacles is not a competition. It is not for us to be braggadocious, nor is it for us to keep tally among our peers.

In full vulnerability, I have come to the realization that most of my competitiveness is against myself. I'm constantly trying to prove to myself that I can do it, when in reality, I don't need to prove anything to anyone, not even myself. God knows exactly what I am capable of because He is the one who made me and continues to mold me. The quest for our own approval puts our eyes on our own abilities and not what God can and is doing through us. So as we go on this journey to overcome obstacles within our ministry, we can, with Godly confidence, say, "Hold my glitter!" I KNOW that God will help me overcome! Watch Him shine!

How do you feel when someone says you can't do something?

Do you find that you are really competitive?

Who are you competing against?

Are you ready to bolster that Godly confidence and say, "Hold my glitter!"?

Glitter

I like to think that I can do things on my own. I don't want to depend on anyone for anything. I have found out the hard way that this is not necessarily a good quality to have. In 2021, I moved to a different state with a new ministry to which God had led me to. I knew no one. Because of my role and position in the church, many people knew who I was; however, I didn't really know them. Excited about my new ministry, I dug right in working with my staff, my volunteers, the kids, and their families. Everything was work, work, work, work…and that's how I liked it. I would take time out for my relationship with God; however, my relationships with everyone else remained surface. I would be there to help them and lead them and love them; however, I did not allow anyone to reciprocate. I didn't have time for relationships, and they were not a priority for me.

Fast forward two years…still no relationships. I knew everyone and everyone knew me, and that was the extent of it. I would encourage others to be in relationships, yet I didn't feel the need. God really began to get ahold of my heart. I joined a ladies' Bible study and began to foster relationships. God put me in a place where I was surrounded by wonderful people, and it was time for me to stop being so stubborn and stop trying to do everything on my own. Although this was difficult for me at first, I was starting to see why it was so important.

In the fall of 2023, I was having a few small issues with my health, and I realized that I hadn't been to a doctor since I had moved. I made an appointment for a physical and was determined to get myself healthy. As you may know, there are many facets to a physical as a woman. It includes a mammogram and time at the gynecologist. I did all the things and thought nothing of it until I got a phone call from the doctor telling me that my mammogram had showed an abnormality that required further testing. Twenty-two years prior to this I was diagnosed with stage 3 breast cancer. I had undergone surgery and very aggressive chemotherapy and radiation. In my mind, the mammogram was merely showing some kind of scar tissue or weird blip. It had been 22 years with no reoccurrence.

A week later I was at The KidzMatter Conference. I was in the green room because I had just been interviewed on stage about the release of my first book. My heart was so full. I had worked so hard for this accomplishment. I felt that God was smiling down on me saying, "Way to go, Debbie! I knew you could do it!" My phone rang, and I noticed it was my doctor. I answered the phone to hear my doctor say the words, "Debbie, you have breast cancer." Wait! What? Talk about whiplash.

The following days were a whirlwind of appointments and decision-making. This was a ginormous obstacle I was facing. I was scared, overwhelmed, and angry. It was decided that a full mastectomy with reconstruction would be the best option for me. Knowing that the upcoming surgeries, treatments, and recovery would take a toll and I would be down for a while, my husband took me away on a trip to Colorado the week before the surgery. Neither of us had ever been to Colorado, and we were excited to see all the mountains and the nature there. It was on this trip that I learned about the aspen trees.

You will never see an aspen tree alone. They are always in a grove with many other trees. Unlike other trees that have their own set of roots, aspen trees share a root system. These amazing trees communicate with each other through their roots. If one tree is not getting enough water, it says, "Hey, I need some water," and the other trees send it water through their root system. If one of the trees gets sick and is not doing well, the other trees pull together and send the sick tree what it needs to get better. When I learned this, I was overwhelmed. God, in all His wisdom, knowing how visual I am, took me to Colorado to give me this beautiful picture of community. A community that held each other up. It wasn't just a one-way relationship. They all thrived…TOGETHER!

As you get to know me, you will learn that I love glitter…a lot! In my opinion, glitter should be used on everything. The sparkle and shine of it just makes me happy. My love for glitter is well-known among the kids within my ministry. On Sundays, it is common for a child to come running up to me to show off their glittery shoes or sparkly dress. I have many pairs of shoes that are "glittery," and I am usually wearing them. The child and I will both put a foot out to compare and admire the glimmer.

I am a boy mom, so that stifled my love for glitter as they were growing up. My boys did not appreciate the glittery heart stickers on their lunch bag, nor did they want anything to do with sparkly crafts. When my first grandchild was born, it was a beautiful baby boy. Once a boy mom, always a boy mom. However, two years later this "Gigi" got a granddaughter. Oh, I was so happy and could not wait to share my love for glitter and all things sparkly. However, my daughter-in-law held me at bay. She wanted my sweet granddaughter to choose glitter and sparkly things on her own and did not want it forced upon her. Sigh. I patiently waited, and I am thrilled to share with you that my sweet granddaughter loves glitter! It's so precious to hear her little voice say, "Oooo, sparkles!"

glit·ter
/ˈglidər/
noun
1. a bright shimmering reflected light.

Similar: sparkle, twinkle, glint, gleam, shimmer, glimmer, flicker, brightness, brilliance

Unfortunately, not everyone shares my love for glitter. Throughout my many years in children's ministry, I have been in places that have banned me from using glitter. I know, that's horrific! I have also had volunteers refuse to do certain crafts with the kids because it involved using glitter. I do not understand how someone would not want this fabulous, twinkly substance. I have also recently learned that there is an actual phobia related to glitter. The fear of glitter is called "sparkalaphobia." I can't make this up. Apparently their fears lie in not being able to get rid of the glitter.

Bear with me as I geek out on a few facts about glitter. In 1934, a man named Henry Ruschmann accidently created what we know as modern-day glitter. Just imagine a man named Henry on his farm in New Jersey. He created a machine to help cut glossy photos. His machine would sometimes stutter and would deposit little bits of paper he would call "schnibbles." The little sparkly fragments were pretty cool, so Henry created a machine just to make "schnibbles" out of scraps of plastic. This was going to be his side business to help pay for feeding his cows on the farm. His "schnibble" business became very popular in the 1940's because people were using it to decorate their Christmas trees in lieu of candles. This side business turned into its own thriving company that still exists to this day. There are two main glitter factories in the world today, both located in New Jersey (Corkill, 2023). Can you imagine how fabulous it would be to work at a glitter factory?

The world's love for glitter and sparkly things did not begin in 1934 with a man named Henry. Ancient civilizations would use tiny mica flakes to give their cave painting a bit of sparkle and glow. Egyptians used to also crush up beetles to create a form of glitter (Sharma, 2017).

You don't have to share my love for glitter to understand that there is just something about things that shine and give a brilliant light. We are drawn to it. According to an article published by the Cleveland Clinic, endorphins are hormones that our body produces to help us reduce stress and pain. These endorphins are released when we do pleasurable activities such as exercise, dancing, laughter, doing acts of kindness, and being in the sunlight. The glistening sunlight produces endorphins to help alleviate stress and pain. You know what else glistens? Glitter! The sparkle of the glitter helps produce endorphins! Therefore, glitter can help take away stress and pain. Basically, glitter makes people happy.

Now that we have this knowledge about glitter, let's talk about its role in overcoming obstacles. It's about to take on a whole new meaning. When you think about glitter, think about the things that help you take away stress and pain. Think about the things that remind you of how good God is and that He is with you in your battle. Think about the things that keep you calm, levelheaded, and your thoughts clear. Think about things that keep your eyes on the brilliant light that is God. **This is your glitter.** As you go into a battle to overcome obstacles, it can become overwhelming and taxing. If not careful, we can lose these things: we lose our "glitter." We become beat down by the difficulty and become stressed out, and before we know it, we are second-guessing the goodness of God and questioning our calling.

Imagine a scenario where you have an obstacle you are about to battle. You have the confidence that God is with you because He promises us this in Psalms 46:1 when He says, "God is our refuge and strength, a very ready help in trouble" (NASB). You know that with God, you've got this. So now you turn to a friend and say, "Hold my glitter." Walk beside me and help me hold on to the things that remind me of God's goodness. "Hold my glitter" so I don't lose my mind and stress out on the battle that God is fighting for me. "Hold my glitter" and be ready to remind me of my calling. "Hold my glitter" so I do not become overwhelmed by the pain. Please, "Hold my glitter" so I am not overtaken by this obstacle. "Hold my glitter."

I write all of this as I am walking through this very difficult, sometimes overwhelming obstacle of cancer. I am so grateful for my "glitter-holders" who are cheering me on and not allowing me to give up and to keep fighting. They encourage me and remind me to keep my eyes on the things of God that bring me peace and relief from stress and pain. I am thankful for God's continual nudge for me to be in community with others and foster relationships so I could have someone to "Hold my glitter."

Throughout my ministry, I have encountered many obstacles. Some of them I totally crushed…and some crushed me. Though I may have been crushed, I have never been destroyed, though it may have felt like that for a time. I invite you to lean in as we discuss obstacles that we face in our ministry. Most likely you have experienced or are currently experiencing the obstacles we will consider. Grab your glitter, and let's overcome… together!

Keeping It Real

What are your thoughts on glitter? It's ok if you don't love it as much as I do.

What are some things that are YOUR GLITTER? Things that keep you going during a battle you are trying to overcome.

Who are your glitter-holders?

Obstacles

ob·sta·cle

/ˈäbztək(ə)l/

noun

plural noun: **obstacles**

a thing that blocks one's way or prevents or hinders progress.

I really do not like this word. It even looks weird as I type it out…obstacle. There are many words I could say instead: snag, drawback, deterrent, obstruction, hiccup, barricade, stumbling block, hurdle, fly in the ointment (I think my grandma used this one.), complication, interference…I am sure you could probably add a few to the list. Regardless of what we call it, an obstacle is something that gets in the way. I don't know about you, but I hate that.

Obstacles are inevitable. At the beginning of the movie *A Bug's Life* by Disney, the film transports you deep into the grass giving you the feeling that you are the size of an ant. The grass is all around you and looks to be as tall as trees. The space between each blade of grass is wide. The scene is a group of worker ants walking in a line, each holding a piece of food. The line is flowing according to plan as each ant drops off their food at the designated location and then returns out to collect more food.

Out of the blue, a leaf blowing in the wind falls to the ground dividing the line of worker ants. The ants begin to panic. They don't know what to do. There is a leaf in the way of the line. They have lost their way. The ants become more frantic when the leader ant comes running to the situation and telling the ants not to panic. He assures the ants that it's going to be ok and that they are going to go "around the leaf." The worker ants hesitantly and cautiously walk around the leaf as the leader guides them step by step until they are around the leaf and back in line with the other ants according to plan. Relief falls over the ants as the leader downplays the leaf and says, "This is nothing compared to the twig of '93." I said all of this to say…"leaves happen."

No matter who you are, how much you plan, how much training you have, or what area of ministry you are in, obstacles are going to happen. Some are small, some are big, some are downright catastrophic, but they happen. It all comes down to how we handle them. I will admit that I am guilty of a few freak-outs over obstacles. I have had temper tantrums (usually in my head, but that still counts) when things do not go according to my plan. I have pouted. I have shut down. I have panicked. I have had moments where I completely lost myself in my quest to overcome an obstacle.

Experience and maturity have taught me to stop fighting the obstacles and learn from them. Obstacles are not necessarily bad: they are opportunities to grow. I have wrestled with God many times through my reluctance to grow and learn. I just want God to fix it and "lead me around the leaf." That's an easy mindset to fall into. When we just search for a quick fix or expect God to come down from heaven in all His splendor and use His powers to just blast the obstacle away, we fail to learn, and we fail to grow. Obstacles shape us into the men and women God intends for us to be. They strengthen our faith and give us character; therefore, our attitude towards obstacles may determine our success in overcoming them. Dare I say that obstacles are good? Eh, I wouldn't go that far.

Expecting obstacles is not a bad thing. However, if you are not careful, you will develop an attitude of doom and gloom. Have you ever heard yourself say, "Well, I just know something is going to ruin this."? "Nothing ever works according to plan, so why do I even bother?" "Why does everything always happen to me?" Sound familiar? This type of attitude sets you up for defeat before you even get out of the gate. Besides, nobody wants to be around a "Debbie Downer." This sort of attitude will send your staff and volunteers running for the hills.

It is important to be vigilant so as not to inadvertently allow room for obstacles. I like to call these self-induced situations. Self-induced situations can be caused by lack of planning, procrastination, disorganization, or oversight. Examples of this would be waiting to the last minute to order things you need for VBS because you kept "forgetting" and now what you need is out of stock. A self-inflicted situation. Planning a family event and making the decision to just "go with the flow" and not plan enough activities. Then the kids and families become bored and frustrated, so they decide to leave. Self-inflicted situation. Or being so disorganized in your storage areas that you purchase a bunch of supplies that you know you have but you can't find, and now you are over your budget. Self-inflicted situation.

I consider myself a planner. When I say a "planner," I mean I like things planned out to the smallest detail. Being in ministry as long as I have, I have learned to expect obstacles. I don't welcome them, but I expect them. My goal has become to plan things to the smallest detail, to consider any potential obstacles, plan alternatives, and do whatever I can to not give room for obstacles to get in my way. If obstacles come, it won't be because I didn't plan well. That is well and good, but as you can see, there sure is a lot of focus on me and my abilities. When God revealed this to me, I was quite humbled. Actually a lot humbled. We will talk more about this later.

I think I may have inherited my overzealous ways to ensure there are no obstacles from my mom. As an adult, I never lived close to my mom. We usually lived across the country from each other. The couple of times a year that I would get to go visit, there is one thing that really stood out…her lawn. Her acre-and-a-half lawn was so green and so lush. Like, REALLY green and REALLY lush. Imagine the most beautiful lawn, that would be my mom's. My kids loved playing in her yard barefoot because there were no "picky" things to poke their feet. It was soft and luxurious. Yes, I am calling grass luxurious. Because we lived so far away, my mom and I talked on the phone often. It was very common for me to call her, and she would answer the phone and be out of breath. She would say, "Sorry. I was pulling weeds." It became a joke in our family. Whenever someone was out of breath for any reason, we would say, "You must have been pulling weeds."

Mom was an empty nester and had now dedicated all her time to her yard; however, I didn't realize how boundless this dedication was. When she would tell me she had been pulling weeds, I would imagine how we pulled weeds as kids. We did not have a weed eater, so we would go along the fence line and pull all the weeds by hand. It was quite the laborious chore that none of the kids liked to do. This is what I imagined her doing.

On one visit to Mom's house, I woke up early to find Mom walking out in her yard. However, this was not just a pleasant stroll through her yard. She was on a mission. She had started at one corner of her yard, and she would walk in a straight line with her head down looking for anything that even resembled a weed. If she found something, she would pull it out and discard it in a bag she had on her arm. When she would get to the end of that "row," she would turn around and go back down the next row doing the same thing. My mom had created a grid in her head for her entire acre-and-a-half lawn and would walk it inch by inch looking for weeds. She did this every day. No wonder she had the best lawn ever. She saw weeds as obstacles interfering with her lush, beautiful lawn, and she was going to do whatever it took to ensure NO WEEDS got in the way.

Mom is in heaven with Jesus now. If she came to my house and saw my lawn, she would be horrified. If you pulled all the weeds out of my lawn, it would be just dirt left. As I said previously, I am a visual person, and God knows that. One day several years ago God gave me a visual to help me understand something that I will never forget. Every day my mom would go inch by inch and look for weeds and remove them. That is what God wants us to do in our lives. We need to take time each day and go inch by inch through our heart looking for things that may impede our walk with Jesus. Things that may trip us up and destroy us.

We are reminded of this in Hebrews 12:1-2, "Therefore, since we also have such a great cloud of witnesses surrounding us, let's rid ourselves of every obstacle and the sin which so easily entangles us, and let's run with endurance the race that is set before us, looking only at Jesus,

the originator and perfecter of the faith…"
(NASB). As leaders in ministry, we are being
watched by those we lead. They are watching to
see how we handle obstacles that come our way.
Not only that, those watching us also see any
self-induced situations because we didn't "pull
the weeds" in our life.

Obstacles are hard and not fun. Some-
times it is difficult to see any glimmers of glitter
through the obstacle, more or less a lesson of
growth or opportunity. You may be reading
this and going through an obstacle that has you
rethinking your ministry or even your calling.
My friend, I am here to encourage you to not
give up.

Keeping It Real

What obstacles are you trying to overcome in your life right now?

When you encounter an obstacle, what is usually your first reaction? What is your attitude toward it?

How often do you find yourself in self-induced situations?

When is the last time you looked your heart over inch by inch to ensure that there are no "weeds" getting in the way?

Are you ready to overcome? Let's keep reading.

Overcoming

o·ver·come
/ˌōvərˈkəm/
verb
present participle: **overcoming**
succeed in dealing with (a problem or dif-
ficulty), defeat (an opponent), prevail, get
the better of, conquer, trounce, vanquish.

We are blessed to have our church on a very large property in central Tennessee. It is absolutely beautiful with the trees, two ponds, a river, and a lot of land. Our youth group takes advantage of the awesomeness by hosting our middle school and high school camps on the property each summer. I had only been on staff for a month when the middle school ministry had their camp. As a staff member, it was really cool to see all the camp excitement going on each day.

On one of the days during that camp, the middle school leaders had rented a ginormous inflatable slide. The middle schoolers put out a challenge for the staff to join them at the slide for races. The kid's team staff, of course, jumped at this opportunity. We made our way to where the slide was set up, and I suddenly felt ill. This slide was literally the biggest, tallest, steepest slide I had ever seen…and I am terrified of heights.

I had already committed to this challenge; I can't back down now. This was more about my pride because my staff was still getting to know me. I couldn't appear to be weak. So I gave myself a pep talk, smiled, and proceeded to climb up to the top of the slide. My pep talk was working because I just focused on the steps and rope in front of me, and I scaled it rather quickly. I was pretty proud of myself…until….

I reached the top. At the top of the slide, you could see straight down, AND it was enclosed at the top so you didn't fall off the top. My pep talk came to a screeching halt as I found myself up so high and in a tight space. Oh, yeah. I'm also claustrophobic.

I'm sitting at the top of the slide to go down, and I freeze in a panic but trying to pretend that I wasn't in a panic. That is no easy feat. The slide was made for three people to go down at once. I was sitting at the top of one lane, and the middle schoolers continued to come and slide down next to me. After many people came up and down the slide, my staff at the bottom of the slide began to realize that something was wrong. They would shout encouragement up to me, and I would shout back that I was fine, I was just letting them go ahead of me. I didn't fool anyone. They all knew I was faking it.

As I sat at the top, I had two choices: plummet to the bottom of this cliff (slide) or propel myself back down the slide with the rope I climbed up on. I decided to just sit there…for, like, ten minutes. The sweetest middle school boy named Jackson decided that he was going to encourage me and stay with me. (This was very embarrassing. I'm supposed to be the encouraging one, and now I'm being encouraged by a middle schooler.)

During those ten minutes, that felt like ten hours, a couple other boys who were jumping down the slide in front of me jumped really hard and almost knocked me down. The bounce they made frightened me as I grabbed on tightly so as not to go down the slide. With my death grip, I inadvertently said a word that was extremely inappropriate. Yes, I said a cuss word…out loud…at church…in front of a middle schooler. I was appalled, and I immediately began apologizing to my new friend, Jackson. I asked him to forgive me and stressed how wrong it was, etc. His exact words were, "Ms. Debbie, it's really no big deal. You should hear the stuff that comes out of my dad's mouth." This did not make me feel better.

I finally realized that I just needed to slide down the slide. With Jackson cheering me on, I was going to close my eyes, count to three, and go for it. One… two… SHOVE! Before I could get to three, Jackson had shoved me down the slide. I went down screaming at the top of my lungs as I awkwardly turned sideways and landed in the side crevice of the slide and was now stuck. Of course, it was all captured on video. My staff and the other kids were cheering me on and high-fiving me as if I had just won a medal.

It was over. I did it. I went down the slide. It was a ginormous obstacle for me, and I did it. However, I may have finally gone down the slide, but I did NOT overcome anything. I still am terrified of heights, I'm still claustrophobic, and the only thing I learned from that experience is to avoid inflatable slides for the rest of my life… and not to cuss (especially in front of middle schoolers).

Obstacles can be really frightening. They are overwhelming and fill us with doubt, fear, and anxiety, among other not-so-pleasant things. Obstacles in ministry can also be disarming. We go into ministry and expect it to be rainbows, butterflies, and glitter. Unfortunately, we soon realize that humans in the church are just that…human. Your brain is now trying to reconcile this reality which makes the obstacle all the more difficult.

When you are faced with an obstacle, you do have choices. You can run from it and decide not to deal with it. You can ignore it and pretend it doesn't exist. You can close your eyes and hope for the best until it's over. You can be dragged through it kicking and screaming. You can be shoved through it. You can allow it to crush you. You can actually OVERCOME it. Unfortunately, I can say I've made all of these choices at one time or another. It's so easy to get to the point where we want to be pushed through it to just get it over. Let me just close my eyes, scream, and awkwardly be shoved through the obstacle. We can also pray and beg God to just remove the obstacle. All that matters is that it's over… until the same obstacle rears its ugly head again.

When we are faced with obstacles in ministry, our goal is to OVERCOME the obstacles. By "overcome," I mean we face it, we deal with it, and we conquer it. When we truly overcome, we learn lessons that grow us as leaders. We become stronger, wiser, and braver. I will be the first to say that this is tough and hard work. However, I will also be the first to say that it is absolutely worth it. As I look back on my years of ministry, I can see where obstacles that would have downright crushed me five years ago, I can now face with confidence and grace. This is because I chose not to close my eyes and hope for the best. I chose to do the work.

At the last church I ministered at, I was there for over ten years. I got the privilege to be a part of the church as it grew from one campus to four campuses in only two years. It was crazy, yet so exciting. We were growing faster than our processes, and we were faced with obstacle after obstacle. It was a great problem to have, and, as a staff, we were working together to overcome these obstacles of growth. In 2016, *Outreach Magazine* named us the #6 Fastest Growing Church in America. Wow!!! It was such a cool honor. We knew God was doing incredible things, but then our bubble was burst…big time.

Soon after we received the award for the #6 Fastest Growing Church in America from *Outreach Magazine*, everything came to a screeching halt. One of our Pastor's sons, who was on staff at the church, was arrested for having inappropriate relations with a minor. The wind was completely knocked out of me. The details of what happened were devastating and would require another book.

As you can imagine, this was absolutely catastrophic. We now were dealing with the heartbreak of what happened to this young girl plus media parked out in our parking lot and trying to stop us as we drove in. Our church name was completely tarnished in the community, and our Pastor was trying to lead the church while also trying to love and support his son. We found out there were other victims. It was five years of dealing with a church split, closing campuses, mega financial hardships, staff layoffs, court cases, families and friends divided. It was horrible. I prayed diligently for God to release me from the church. "Please, God. Send me somewhere else! I do not know how to deal with this, nor do I want to. This is too much!!!" Family members were continually telling me to get out and to leave; however, I never felt that God was releasing me. Even though no one would have faulted me for leaving, I knew that God wanted me right where I was. I stayed.

Most churches would not have survived this type of devastation, but God had other plans. We fought and fought, and after several years, we started to see the dust settle and the clouds clear. The church got a breath of fresh air and started to grow again. This time with processes in place. A true beauty-from-ashes example. Then God said, "Debbie, I release you." "What???? Now that it's getting good again, now you say it's ok to go?" We don't always understand what God is doing, but His plans are perfect.

In 2021, I moved across the country to the new ministry God led me to. I have to say it was the most refreshing feeling. I was now at a vibrant, growing church that was beloved in the community. I remember walking around the property shortly after I got there just thanking and praising God for allowing me to experience this goodness. Two months later the church encountered disastrous events that led to a church split. My exact words were, "Come on,

God! Seriously????" As clear as day, I heard God say, "This is why I brought you here." From that moment on, I planted my feet and got to work leading my team through this devastating obstacle. Guess what? Although it was difficult, I was confident, not fearful, and not shaken.

All obstacles are different; therefore there are many ways to go about overcoming. However, when you decide to take your obstacle head on, there are a few things I want to encourage you with:

1. **Remember that you are not alone.** "You keep track of all my sorrows. You have collected all my tears in your bottle. You have recorded each one in your book. My enemies will retreat when I call to you for help. This I know: God is on my side! I praise God for what he has promised; yes, I praise the Lord for what he has promised. I trust in God, so why

should I be afraid?..." Psalms 56:8-11 (NLT)

2. **Slow down to experience God.** "Be still, and know that I am God!..." Psalms 46:10 (NLT)

3. **Pray for wisdom.** "But the wisdom from above is first of all pure. It is also peace loving, gentle at all times, and willing to yield to others. It is full of mercy and the fruit of good deeds. It shows no favoritism and is always sincere. And those who are peacemakers will plant seeds of peace and reap a harvest of righteousness." James 3:17-18 (NLT)

4. **Handle it with grace.** "Let your conversation be gracious and attractive so that you will have the right response for everyone." Colossians 4:6 (NLT)

5. **Love people through it.** "All praise to God, the Father of our Lord Jesus

Christ. God is our merciful Father and the source of all comfort. He comforts us in all our troubles so that we can comfort others. When they are troubled, we will be able to give them the same comfort God has given us." 2 Corinthians 1:3-4 (NLT)

6. **Recognize and celebrate the wins.** "But I will give repeated thanks to the Lord, praising him to everyone." Psalm 109:30 (NLT)

7. **Look for lessons to learn.** "The godly may trip seven times, but they will get up again. But one disaster is enough to overthrow the wicked." Proverbs 24:16 (NLT)

When the odds are stacked against you, when the obstacles seem monumental and the outcome looks to be impossible, just remember, it may be impossible for us…but not for God. That is just so cool. Hand off that glitter!

Keeping It Real

How do you normally go about dealing with obstacles?

How many times have you closed your eyes and hoped for the best? Or prayed for God to just blast away the obstacle?

What lessons have you learned by the obstacles you have overcome?

Our Calling

Before we dive into overcoming specific obstacles in ministry, I feel I need to stop and talk about our calling. I want you to take some time and think back to when you were called to do ministry. For some, it was a powerful moment where you felt God's leading, but for others, it may have just happened slowly until one day you realized that you were doing something bigger than yourself. Regardless of how or when you were called into ministry, I want to remind you that when God calls you, He calls you. He selected YOU to be within a certain ministry at a certain time for a reason.

I have quit ministry at least 10,463 times… in my head. There have been countless days where I go home after a tough Sunday and just cry. It will be determined in my brain that on Monday I am handing in my resignation. Monday comes, and I don't. I don't actually quit because I learned a long time ago that the calling that God put on my life is purposeful. It is an honor because not everyone gets to do what I do. Yes, there are days that are really dreadful. However, I get to lead kids to Jesus. I get to help form their biblical worldview. I get to walk with families during their most vulnerable moments. I get to celebrate milestones with them. I get to be a part of something bigger than me. Wow!

The enemy wants nothing more than to take you out. He wants you to doubt your calling and forfeit what God is doing through you. He will throw every obstacle he can to take you out. I challenge you…please, do not forget your calling. Out of all the people in all the world, God called YOU to minister where you are. It's time to say, "Hold my glitter 'cause I've got some obstacles to overcome!"

Keeping It Real

When did God call you to ministry?

Have you ever tried to quit? Even if it was in your head?

What made you to not quit?

Take a moment and consider that God called YOU to be right where you are…on purpose.

Hold My Glitter as I Overcome the Obstacle of "Me"

With a lot of self-assessment, I came to the conclusion that I am my biggest obstacle. I often doubt myself and my abilities. I overthink things…a lot. It's very easy for me to cop an attitude…but not show it. If there was an Olympic sport for putting yourself down, I would have the gold medal. This is an obstacle that I continue to tackle and overcome. The sad thing is a lot of times it's an obstacle that no one ever sees or even realizes because I got really good at disguising it. To overcompensate for my self-doubt lack of confidence, I would become obsessed with making the perfect plan and doing things MY way. If things did not go my way, I would throw a mega temper tantrum…in my head.

God showed me that I sure did put a lot of focus on myself. I focused so much on what I could do and what I couldn't do, etc. I was consumed with thoughts of myself. Most of the time they were not positive thoughts, but they were still all about me. This left little room to love others.

Once I realized that my mind was causing me a lot of trouble, I began to pray every morning to get myself in the right frame of mind. I would constantly be quoting Philippians 4:8 where it says, "… Fix your thoughts on what is true, and honorable, and right, and pure, and lovely, and admirable…are excellent and worthy of praise" (NLT). This was my mind filter. If it wasn't true, I wasn't allowed to think about it. If it wasn't honorable, I wasn't allowed to think about it. I would go through the whole list. I will say that this really works. If you have trouble with your mind being all wonky, I highly recommend this.

Being in ministry, Sundays are our big day, of course. At the height of battling the obstacle of me, I had such a great desire to take my mind and attitude captive and be truly sincere to the team I led and to the kids and families that I served. I wanted to focus on others and not myself. On the way to church, my prayer each week would be, "Lord, help me to truly love, help me to truly listen, and, Lord, help me to recognize anyone around me that needs a special touch from you. This is not about me; it's all about you."

Several years ago, it was the day we were opening our fourth campus in two years. This was a really big deal. I prayed my prayer on the way to church and was ready to rock out the day. Everything was going smoothly, and there was excellence everywhere you looked. I will say I was pretty proud of myself. With this being the fourth campus that I was a part of opening, I felt very confident. As the end of the service was coming to a close, I was walking through the kid's area one last time to check on things.

Before I continue on with this story, I need to stop right here and set the stage. This was a portable campus at a high school. We set most of the kid's ministry up in a very large cafeteria as well as a few nearby classrooms. We used play panels and pipe and drapes to create classrooms for the preschool area. My husband would lovingly call it the "petting zoo" because he could look in and reach down and pet the head of a child. Anyway, when you entered the kid's ministry area, you would turn right and see all the portable classrooms on each side of you. To pick up any age child, you had to go this way. If you walked into the kid's area and went straight, you would run into our Clubhouse Ministry.

Our Clubhouse Ministry is a ministry that we had for the families of staff and volunteers with children who would be at both services because they were serving. It was a safe, unstructured environment that the kids would go to during the second service. During the first service, they would attend their classes, and then the Clubhouse team would pick them up and take them to Clubhouse where they had lunch, played, and hung out together. The goal is to allow parents with children to serve, however, ensuring that the kids don't start hating church because they were always there. The kids LOVED Clubhouse! Like I said, if you walked into our kid's ministry and went straight, you would run right into Clubhouse. This was another area that everyone picking up their child would pass by. Clubhouse was set up in a very wide hallway with play panels.

Now back to the story. I was making my final round through the kid's area. I walked over to Clubhouse, looked over the play panels, and I noticed that the leaders and all the kids were at the far end of the Clubhouse area watching a movie. However, one three-year-old little girl was playing all by herself at a table on the side closest to the entrance. Upon closer look, I noticed what the child was playing with. I opened the gate and ran inside of Clubhouse. This sweet little precious girl, Darla, wanted to finger paint. However, she didn't have any finger paint, so she improvised.

Apparently Darla had pooped in her Pull-Up. She reached down into the backside of her Pull-Up and pulled out her hand full of poop and was finger painting on the table. This was quite the masterpiece. She made swirls and letters and covered every inch of the table. Darla then decided that the play panels needed to be painted as well, so she "finger painted" those. If she ran out of "paint," she would just put her hand into her backside and pull out some more. She noticed that her chair didn't have any "paint" on it, so she included that into her project. By the time I found her, sweet little Darla had just reloaded her hand with "paint" and was gliding her hands up and down the table legs. She was determined not to miss a spot anywhere.

I must take another pause before I go on to the next part of this story. I want to remind you about my prayer earlier in the day. The awesome thing about God is that He gives us the desires of our hearts. He knew I wanted to love well. He made sure the Holy Spirit was right there with me to act as my filter as I responded to this…"art project." Along the way, I will be giving what I said in my humanness and how the Holy Spirit filtered it and what actually came out of my mouth.

As I entered Clubhouse, I got the attention of the leaders to show them what they were missing and asked them what was going on.

> *Debbie's humanness: "What in the world are you all doing???"*
> *Holy Spirit filter: "Um, ladies, we have a situation over here."*

I went over to Darla to move her away from the table to get her to cease her "finger painting." As I moved her, she grabbed onto my leg with her hands, and now my skirt is, yes, covered in poop. The Clubhouse ladies came running over to me and literally just stood there staring at me and Darla in disbelief. I think I heard them trying to apologize; however, I had other things on my mind.

Just then, the church service let out, and all the parents were now walking towards the kid's ministry...past Clubhouse. As I looked down at Darla, I got to see the full scope of the situation. There was poop all up and down her arms, all over her dress, on her legs, on her face, and in her hair. The Clubhouse leaders were still just standing there looking at me. I instructed them to take care of the other children as they were being picked up, and I would clean up Darla and the "finger paint." I didn't want to walk any further and spread the poop, so I asked the leaders to get me the wipes and cleaning supplies. They replied with, "We don't know where the cleaning supplies are."

Debbie's humanness: *"How do you not know? You are the ones who set up this area."*

Holy Spirit filter: *"They are in the bin under the teacher table."*

Parents were walking by and rubbernecking trying to see what was happening. They knew it wasn't good as they were getting hit with the thick scent of poop. Now that I had baby wipes, I got down on my knees to be level with Darla to make it easier for me to clean her up. Darla is a very loving and affectionate child. When I got down on my knees to get closer to her, she assumed it was time for hugs and snuggles. This sweet precious, darling little girl wrapped her arms around my neck and squeezed me so tight. Her hands stroked my hair as she smiled. I was desperately trying to lovingly clean her hands first to stop the dissemination of the poop. The more feverishly I worked to get the poop off Darla, the more poop got on me. She squirmed and wiggled and at one point decided to sit down on my knees. May I remind you that this was all going on during parent pickup time.

I asked for the leaders to please go get Darla's momma. After what felt like an eternity, momma came nonchalantly strolling into Clubhouse. She looked down at me and Darla, looked over at the "finger paint masterpiece," and laughed! Yes, she laughed and said, "Oh, you know three-year-olds."

> **Debbie's humanness:** *"No, no. I don't know three-year-olds! Not like this!"*
> **Holy Spirit filter:** *(Mouth remained shut and passed off Darla with a smile.)*

Right there in the middle of Clubhouse, during parent pickup, momma lifted up the dress of Darla and took it off of her. We now have a naked three-year-old, covered in poop, just standing there for all to see.

Debbie's humanness: "Um, NO, you are not going to do this here. Take her to the bathroom."

Holy Spirit filter: I'm going to agree with Debbie at this point. What she said.

Momma once again walked nonchalantly through the entire kid's ministry to the bathroom with naked little Darla by her side. I looked down at myself. I was literally covered in poop. My clothes had poop smeared all over them. I had poop in my hair, on my face, in my ears, and I know it must have been in my nose because that is all I could smell. In fact, sometimes I think I can still smell it to this day.

With Darla now with her momma, I began the task of cleaning up the poop masterpiece she left behind. Y'all, I can't even tell you how many times I dry-heaved during this process. What made this task even more difficult is that we were at a portable campus and everything needed to be taken down and packed into a trailer until the next week. I was racing to clean up the poop and sanitize everything before it was taken away.

I finally completed the cleanup and walked to the bathroom to try to clean myself up so I could get into my car without spreading the poop any farther. As I walked into the bathroom, I saw sweet Darla, naked, standing under a hand dryer. Momma had "washed" her hair out in the sink. Momma had a Pull-Up and an oversized t-shirt that one of my staff had found for her to put on Darla to get her home. She looked over at me as I was trying to wipe the poop off of my face and said, "You know, you really should have extra clothes on hand for times like these. Now I have to take Darla to the restaurant like this."

> **Debbie's humanness:** *"Seriously? At least you still get to go to the restaurant. I'm going to have to strip down just to get into my car."*

Holy Spirit filter: *"You are absolutely right. I will work on that."*

Fast forward three years. It was my last week at this church before I moved across the country to my new ministry. As I stood in the church lobby, this momma was standing right by me along with several other people. Momma was thanking me and telling me how much she was going to miss me. She proceeded to tell the group of people standing with us the story of what happened with Darla. I had never heard the story from her point of view. She told the others how I handled it so calmly and that I was so loving and sweet even though I was covered in poop. I was blown away because that was definitely not how I remembered it. God did that. He allowed me to love despite my human-ness. He sent the Holy Spirit to filter my words and my attitude, and I know it was because I prepared my heart and mind that morning. I was able to take my mind off of myself and just love.

That's not all God did. Because my humanness did not take over during the poop situation, it opened a line of communication between Darla's momma and myself. In the months following, it had been revealed that Darla had special needs. Darla had been born not able to hear and wasn't able to have surgery to correct it until age two. This delayed her speech significantly and, unfortunately, other difficulties came along with this. Darla's momma really struggled with accepting the diagnosis, just as any momma would. She fought hard for Darla to be treated "normal" and did not want any accommodations for her. I got to walk alongside the family as we together created a plan and accommodations to ensure Darla was safe and that she was getting to learn about Jesus in a way that she could understand.

The obstacle of "me" is very dangerous. It can make or break your ministry. The enemy knows that if he can just plant a seed of doubt or anger or discouragement or frustration in your mind, you will do the damage yourself. Taking time to self-assess where you are with the obstacle of "me" is important. Sometimes we don't realize that we are the problem because we are focused on the wrong thing. We have enough obstacles against us in ministry. The last thing we need is to destroy our own ministry. You know what to say, "Hold my glitter! I'm gonna crush the obstacle of 'me'."

Keeping It Real

Are you encountering the obstacle of "me"?

Take some time to self-assess. What is God showing you that you need to deal with?

How is it affecting your ministry?

What is God leading you to do or change to tackle the obstacle of "me"?

Ok. I have to ask… do you have a poop story?

Hold My Glitter as I Overcome the Obstacle of Perception

As I talk to children's ministry leaders, I notice that there is a universal frustration. We get frustrated when we work so hard to create programs and teach kids about Jesus and disciple them, yet people call it childcare or babysitting. Their perception is that kid's church is just a place for them to drop off their kids to play and hang out so the parents can go into the main service where THEY can learn about Jesus. We know that we are helping kids form their biblical worldview. Yet, they see childcare. Many years ago, in an attempt to overcome the obstacle of perception, I had t-shirts made for my volunteer team. On the back of the shirt, it said:

BABYSITTING?
We don't sit on babies.

It was funny and people laughed. It made them pause a moment to think about it; however, it did not change their perception. A t-shirt or our correcting people when they say "childcare" will not change perception. This obstacle can be overwhelming when you see that parents, other people in the church, church staff, the pastor, and even your volunteers have a warped perception of what children's ministry is and what we do.

The good thing about this is perception can be changed. It will not happen overnight. It takes diligence, commitment, and time. When you crush this obstacle, not only will people take notice, but it will also make you more attractive to volunteers.

First of all, you need to understand that EVERYTHING you do plays into how your ministry is perceived.

- The vision that is cast
- The culture that is set
- The behavior that is allowed
- The details that are focused on
- The appreciation shown
- The resources provided
- The safety protocols that are put into place
- The communication made both internally and externally
- The partnerships with families

I could go on and on. However, did you notice that I didn't say anything about curriculum, programming, and the décor of the Children's Ministry area? You can have the most amazing curriculum and programming and spend thousands of dollars on the coolest, state-of the-art facility and still have a ministry that is perceived as childcare. Yes, these things are important. However, many children's ministry leaders put all their focus solely on these things and not realize there is so much more.

Here are five things that will ruin the perception of your ministry. You may not think that people notice these things, but they do. Not only can these things ruin the perception, but they could also cost you future volunteers.

1. Grumbly Volunteers

The best recruiter and perception setter for your ministry is a happy, purpose-filled volunteer. The best deterrent is a grumbly one. Frustrated, overwhelmed volunteers who lack vision can kill a ministry...and quick. It is important to ensure that your team has a safe place to voice their concerns and frustrations. If they don't have it with you or your leadership team, they will voice their concerns elsewhere. Most likely they are not intentionally trying to cause harm; however, a grumbly volunteer can be quite toxic.

2. An Unorganized Ministry

Children's ministry can be a bit chaotic at times. However, if parents or volunteers see leadership in a constant state of chaos, it can be repelling. If you or the leadership team never seem to have it all together, can't seem to find things, are always running behind, or the class-rooms and storage rooms are unkept and trashy, it can send the best of volunteers running for the hills. Not to mention that it gives parents and others the perception that you are too over-whelmed to care for their child.

3. Low or No Standards

When volunteers are scarce, it's tempting to allow just anyone onto your children's min-istry team. However, low standards or no stan-dards within a ministry keeps your high-quality volunteers away. Examples of low or no stan-dards would be volunteers showing up late or not showing up at all and not dealing with it, or broken policies and procedures that are never dealt with. Or maybe you have "written standards," but you don't enforce them. This is not just seen internally. Parents do notice these things as well.

4. A "Needy" Ministry

This is a tough one. There is a fine line between expressing the need for more volunteers and appearing needy. No one intends to appear "needy." However, if in your recruiting you use phrases like the following, people may see your ministry as "needy."

> *"I'm begging you…"*
> *"We desperately need you…"*
> *"Please, please, please…"*
> *"I'm drowning…"*
> *"No one wants to help…"*

These statements may be true -- maybe you are drowning and you do desperately need them -- however, if you are not careful, you will end up with a "woe-is-me" attitude about your ministry. It is possible to recruit without appearing "needy." It's all in the way you cast the vision for your ministry. It's a privilege to serve in children's ministry, and not just anyone can do it. People may and probably will respond to the "needy" plea…but they won't stay.

5. Shame and Guilt and a Bad Attitude

In attempt to help recruit volunteers for children's ministry, I have seen pastors guilt and shame people from the pulpit. Some have even gone so far as to make videos in dark children's ministry rooms saying, "These rooms will be closed if you do not volunteer." Guilt and shame can be impactful, and, yes, people will respond. However, they will definitely not stay. A bad attitude about how you feel under resourced or not seen will only further damage the perception of your ministry.

Now let's talk about what changes perception in a positive way. Not only will these things allow people to see your ministry differently, but they will attract the quality volunteers you want on your team.

1. High Standards/Excellence

It is a privilege to serve in children's ministry! Do not accept just anyone. When people start hearing that others are getting turned away from serving on the kid's team…things will shift!

Ensure excellence in EVERYTHING you do. A few years ago I had a team of volunteers working at the church preparing for an upcoming event. We were stuffing bags for giveaways for all the kids. I had explained how they needed to be done. However, a couple of the ladies sloppily shoved things in the bags, and they were all messy and looked like they had been dropped on the floor and kicked around. I corrected them and re-explained how they needed to be done. One of the ladies replied, "What's the big deal? They're just kids."

WHAT????? Did she really just say that? Oh, yes, she did. I lovingly told them that they are NOT "just kids." Those kids are just as much of a child of God as you are, and we will be just as excellent for them as we would be for the things we do for the adults. The kids may not notice it, but their parents will…and so will God! Needless to say, that situation set the standard from that moment on. Excellence attracts people.

2. Accountability

People actually thrive under accountability. Those who don't like being held accountable will leave the team, and that's what you want. First of all, if you have volunteers on your roster that you cannot count on, take them off the roster and stop scheduling them. It only causes continued frustration and aggravation for you and the other volunteers.

Ensure you are addressing issues such as those who constantly arrive late, volunteers who are not prepared, display grumbling behavior, etc. If you do not address issues, that will become your culture.

While setting a high standard, you may hear a volunteer say, "But I'm just a volunteer." Be sure to reply, "NO! You are not 'just a volunteer.' You have accepted a role where you are privileged to teach kids about Jesus. You, as a volunteer, are helping form their biblical worldview. So, no, you are not 'just a volunteer'." Children's ministry leader, please remember that you have the responsibility to teach these precious kids and YOU have an obligation to set standards and hold people to them...in love, of course.

3. Events With Purpose That WIN

Be careful what you are putting on the calendar. You do not have to pack out everyone's calendar to have a successful children's ministry. In fact, that will probably burn you out and do the opposite. Be selective with the events you choose. Don't fall into the "we-always-do-this-event-so-we-have-to-do-it-again" trap. Every season is different, and it's ok not to always do the same events just because you've always done them. Ensure that every event that is scheduled has a purpose with an expressed win. Then execute it with excellence. No half-hearted events allowed…ever.

4. A Winning Team

Everyone wants to be part of a winning team. Does your team know if and when they are winning? Define the win! Remember that depending on the season your ministry is in, your win may change each week. An example of what a win could be is that every child gets greeted and talked to every single week. That is a great relational win. Another win could be learning memory verses or kids getting saved and baptized. I have had Sundays that have been so rough that our win was to send all the kids home with the correct parents. We joke about it now; however, as a children's ministry leader, I'm sure you can relate.

5. Clear Vision

What is the overall vision of Children's Ministry? Do you have one? Does your volunteer team know your vision? Do the parents know your vision? Does the church staff know your vision? Does the pastor know your vision, and is it aligned with the church? Are the things you do in your ministry things that actually reflect your vision? Vision can help overcome frustrations. If volunteers know the end goal and know what they are striving for, they will stay for the "long haul." If families know your vision, they will be apt to support your ministry.

This shift of mindset is not easy. IT TAKES A LOT OF COURAGE. However, when people start seeing the change, there will be a shift in how your ministry is viewed. It's time to hand over that glitter.

Keeping It Real

How is your ministry perceived?

What part of the perception of others bothers you the most?

How do you want others (parents, people in the church, church staff, pastor) to perceive your ministry?

What steps can you start taking to change the perception, if needed.

Hold My Glitter as I Overcome the Obstacle of Too Much!

Children's ministry is a lot of work. I am not telling you anything that you don't know. There are some days where the to-do list is just too much. It's insurmountable. The load becomes so overwhelming that you begin to despise what you do or you just shut down and take a nap and not do anything at all. While tasks of ministry can take its toll, I have found that most leaders who become overloaded by tasks are usually trying to do it on their own.

In Exodus 18:13-27, we see the first example of leadership delegation. Moses' father-in law, Jethro, came for a visit. He witnessed Moses with the Israelite people. Moses worked from morning to night leading the people, settling disputes, and giving words from God. Jethro told Moses that the job he was doing was way too much for just one man to do and asked him why he was doing it all alone. Moses replied that it was his job. It was the responsibility that God gave him; therefore, he felt it was all on him to get it done. Jethro disagreed and warned Moses that he was going to wear himself out. He did agree that God had given Moses this great responsibility; however, he didn't understand why Moses was doing all the work while his men would just stand around watching him do it. Jethro advised Moses to delegate. He encouraged Moses to select men he could trust and train. Divide the workload among them according to what they can handle. Moses would still be in charge; however, he would only deal with the major issues while his men handled the smaller one.

What an amazing lesson in delegation! Have you been there? "But it's my responsibility, so I have to do all the work."? Yes, it's your responsibility; however, that doesn't mean you are supposed to do it alone. This obstacle of too much was one that took me years to battle. It still rears its ugly head from time to time. However, now that I have experienced the joys of delegating, it doesn't take much to get me back on track.

The first thing you need to do is figure out why you choose not to delegate. Self-assessment time: it's time to get real and be honest with yourself. Here are some popular reasons why leaders choose not to delegate.

- It's easier to do it by myself.
- I don't have time to teach anyone how to do it.
- No one can do it as good as me.
- I don't trust anyone.
- What if they do it better than me and they end up taking my job?
- You love doing it and don't want to give it up.

Does any of this sound familiar? You may find that your excuse is valid; however, it is also valid that if you do not delegate and remain buried under a hefty to-do list, you will limit your ministry and/or burn out. I must also say that if someone does do a task better than you, FANTASTIC! That is what you want, to surround yourself with amazing people. For the record, no one wants your job. And if they do, let them have it because that would mean that God is moving you on to an even greater assignment.

When you choose not to delegate, you limit your ministry. You are basically saying that this is as far as I'm going to let it go. Yikes! You are also limiting your capacity. When you delegate, you create more capacity for you to lead. It allows you to do even more in the ministry. May I remind you that ministry is way more than tasks. It's about people. If you are bogged down by tasks, you have little to no time to actually minister to the people around you.

Also, when you choose not to delegate, you hold back others. Think back to when someone trusted you for the first time and allowed you the opportunity to take on more responsibility. It's your job to do the same, elevate others. There is a popular saying that says, "We rise by elevating others." I can attest that this is a very true statement. It goes without saying, a lack of delegation also leads to burnout. If you burn out, you end up not doing ministry at all. You get to choose.

Let's get started on tackling this obstacle. Here are some tried and true things to help get you started on your delegation journey.

Make a list of EVERYTHING you do within your ministry. This may take you a week or so to complete. Be detailed. List the smallest of things. Everything takes time.

Circle the things that only YOU can do. Now that you have an extensive list of everything you do, examine the list carefully and circle the things that only YOU can do. No, I didn't say circle the things that you WANT to do. There is a difference. This is a big part of the process. It will be difficult because you may have to let go of something you really enjoy. However, remember that you are trading it for things that are even bigger and better.

Pray about to whom you can delegate. So many times I have heard leaders say, "I don't have anyone to delegate to." While there may be a few occasions that this is true, usually there are people. We are just not looking for them. Seek God to guide you to people to ask. They may say no, but they might say yes, and most of the time they do. May I also add to be careful not to say no for them. Don't get it in your head that they are too busy or make an excuse for them before you ask. There have been many times I've seen where the person is elated to be asked and had even been praying for God to lead them to where they could do more.

Schedule time to teach and train. Yes, I know you are probably yelling at the book saying, "But I don't have time to do this!" You must make time to get this delegation process up and running. As you teach, set clear expectations. You can't get upset if they don't do it the way you want it done if you don't tell them what you expect. Be detailed in your explanation. If you want the sticker put in the upper left-hand corner of the page and you left that detail out, you may end up with stickers in the middle of the page. That is on you. It is also very important to explain the why. You need the sticker to go on the upper left-hand corner because you are putting something else in the middle, etc.

Once you have given clear detailed expectations and explained the why, you trust them to get the job done. You need to trust, yet it's ok to verify. Check in to see if they have any questions or to see if they require further explanation. Verify is not the same thing as micromanaging and hovering. Empower them to do the job. Be aware that they may do the job a little differently than you would. That is ok. Allow them to learn and grow in the process.

There may be a time when the task you delegate will end up back in your lap. You will have the urge to just keep it and continue to do it yourself. Do not fall into this trap. You will end up right back where you started... buried.

I'm not going to lie. Learning to delegate can be tough. I have several stories of delegation gone wrong. However, don't give up. I promise you that it is worth it. Once you begin to experience the load lifting and you see others take ownership, you won't want to stop.

Early in my delegation obstacle battle, I encountered a situation where I felt forced to delegate before I was ready. At that time, I was leading the children's ministry at our church. As I was leading all the areas, I continued to lead the second service elementary class. I LOVED this class. As the pastor continued to add responsibilities, I refused to let go of this class. I assured him that I would be fine and I could handle everything and keep my class.

One day he brought me into the office to tell me that we were about to launch our second campus and he wanted me to be the central children's ministry director and lead both campuses. I was thrilled and so honored. However, he said, "Debbie, you are going to now have to let go of the class. This is not a suggestion." I went home that night and was devastated. On one hand, I was excited for this opportunity; however, I did not want to give up my class. I was literally crying when my husband said, "Let me try to understand this. You would rather settle for ministering to 100 kids when God is giving you the opportunity to minister to 1,000? I don't understand the problem." This immediately stopped me in my tracks. He was right. God was increasing my capacity and elevating me, yet I was choosing to settle and limit my ministry. This was the turning point for me.

Let's do this! Let's increase our capacity and expand our ministries while we elevate leaders to join us. If Moses could do it, we can too. I will hold your glitter for you.

How big is the delegation obstacle for you?

Why do you choose not to delegate?

What would you do if you found that you had more capacity?

I challenge you to start making your list today.

Hold My Glitter as I Tackle the Obstacle of Recruiting and Retaining Volunteers -Part 1-

It doesn't matter what size church or what kind of church you are at. We all have something in common -- the need for more volunteers. Just when you think your team is stable, life happens and some of your team must step out for one reason or another. It's a perpetual cycle. Don't take it personally. However, we do have the ability to slow down the cycle. Get your glitter out because you can consider this obstacle overcome!

A pastor friend once asked me how much time I spend each week recruiting volunteers to my team. I didn't quite understand what he was asking me at first, but then I realized he literally wanted to know how many hours I spend recruiting each week. After a few brief seconds, I responded, "I never stop. I am always recruiting for my team." As a fellow children's ministry leader, I am sure you know exactly what I am talking about.

When I was leading the children's ministry while the church was growing so fast (We went from one to four campuses in two years.), I experienced a perpetual cycle of volunteer shortages that almost crushed me. Each week my assistant and I would work on the volunteer schedule together. We were about to open our third campus; however, my volunteer deficit was not covering the two we already had. Each Tuesday my assistant would let me know how many holes we had. Some weeks it was 7, some weeks it was 12, some weeks 18. It would fluctuate depending on the week. I was in full-blown recruit mode; however, I couldn't recruit fast enough to handle the growth. Each week I would exhaust every resource I had. I would pull out my "back-pocket people," the ones I would use only in an emergency. The stress and frustration were dire.

Our pastor had planned for a staff retreat. We were going away for three days together as a staff to bond and be refreshed and do things you do on staff retreats. Normally I would enjoy this type of activity; however, at this time, the thought of being away during this difficult season seemed frivolous and a waste of time. I told my assistant that I would stay available to her via phone so we could text and call back and forth and I could still help her with the schedule.

The retreat was at Capon Springs in West Virginia. Most staff members drove themselves to the retreat, and I was among those who did. The drive was beautiful. It was fall, and the colors were spectacular. Upon arrival, we all quickly found out that there was no internet, no cell service, NOTHING! We were smack-dab in the middle of a dead zone. The pastor said he didn't want to tell us before we got there because he knew we wouldn't come. I was so angry. Not only can I not call my family and check in, but I would also not be able to help my assistant as I promised. I couldn't even tell her I couldn't help her.

At the first session of the staff retreat, our pastor introduced our guest speaker for the retreat. It was someone we were familiar with who had tons of experience and was on staff at a multi-site mega church a few states away. Pastor encouraged us to find time with our guest during the retreat and pick his brain and get the help we needed for our ministry areas. I felt a little glimmer of hope. I was going to make sure I had time with our guest, tell him my struggles, and pray that he has an answer or some kind of special formula for me to conquer this mammoth obstacle.

At two different meals, I positioned myself to be at the same table with our guest. I had my questions and notepad ready to take notes. Both times our pastor sat next to our guest and dominated the conversation the entire time. My glimmer of hope was fading quickly. On the last day of the retreat, I was walking through the property to the final session. All of a sudden, my phone just started dinging. As I was walking, I entered a very rare spot that had cell service and all my missed texts and calls started pouring in. I opened up my phone and saw a message from my assistant. It said, "Debbie, we have 28 holes this week." I was done. I was literally out of answers.

I went to the final session, and at the end, our guest speaker was standing in the middle of the room while several staff members lined up to talk to him and/or ask him questions. Here it is I thought, my one final chance to get a solution to my problem. I got in line. I was the eighth person in line, and there were a couple others behind me. I waited patiently for my turn. My glimmer of hope was starting to sparkle a little. Now I am the next person in line. It's almost my time.

He finished with the person in front of me, looked up, and looked past me as if I wasn't even there and yelled out to a specific group of people to head outside to take a photo. He then just walked away and left me standing there. I was absolutely devastated. I feel I need to add that I know that if this guest knew that he did this, he would feel awful. He's not that kind of person. I think that he just had a lot of people pulling for time with him. Unfortunately, I just happened to be one that was left standing empty.

In disbelief by what had just happened to me, I went over to my seat to gather my things and walked out. I didn't talk to anyone. I didn't tell anyone I was leaving. I just left. As I got outside and was making my way to my vehicle, hot tears streamed down my face. At that point, I made the determination that I was not the one for the job. I had nothing left to give. I got to my car and lost it. I sobbed and sobbed and cried out to God. "God, I thought I heard you correctly. I thought this is what I was meant to do. You have the wrong person." I cried and prayed and screamed and wept the entire hour-and-a-half drive home.

When I got home and was unloading the stuff from my car, I found a book that someone had given me a few weeks prior. I had put it in my car and forgotten about it. The book was *Sun Stand Still* by Steven Furtick. That evening as I was trying to calm down, I picked up the book and began to read it. It was about having audacious prayers. The book detailed the story of Joshua and the Israelite army as they went to battle with the Amorites. Joshua's prayer was so audacious that he asked God to let the sun stand still to give him more daylight so he could defeat the Amorites…and God did it!!!

As I read this, I began to weep yet again, only this time my tears were filled with hope. I finally understood what I needed to do. This whole time I was waiting for a special formula or quick fix to my processes to overcome my vast volunteer deficit; however, what I was missing was audacious prayers. Yes, I had been praying to God, but they certainly were not audacious. If God let the sun stand still for Joshua to win his battle, He would surely do the same for me.

Below are the steps that I took after I had my light bulb moment. I am listing them out in detail in hopes it will help you too.

1. Know exactly what you need.

I was continually saying, "I just need volunteers." However, I didn't really know what I needed. What does that mean? I took the time to figure out what exactly I needed. How many volunteers do I need? What classrooms/age groups do I need them in? I had multiple services, so what service(s) do I need volunteers? Do I need only adult volunteers? Do I need junior volunteers (teenagers)? Do I need men? Do I need women? The more specific I got, the better I understood the scope of what I actually needed. Now I knew what to pray for. I had a number; it was 54. I needed 54 volunteers, and I knew exactly where I needed them to be.

2. Rally the volunteers you currently have.

I shared my audacious prayers with the volunteer team. Everyone knew the number (54), and we all banded together to pray. The team was excited to be a part of the process. We prayed that God would lead us to people to invite them to be on our team.

3. Cast the vision.

As we were given the opportunities to talk to prospective volunteers, we took the time to share the vision of the children's ministry. We shared our hearts to disciple and make a difference in the next generation.

4. Be selective.

We are going to get real with this part. I have been in children's ministry for a very long time. I have been in little churches, megachurches, multi-site churches, and everything in between. We already determined that we all have one thing in common -- the need for more volunteers. I understand how that need can be so great and overwhelming that any "warm body" will do. I made the decision at this moment to raise my standard and be selective.

It is a privilege to serve within a children's ministry. It is not for everyone. Just because someone is willing to "meet a need" and can pass a background check doesn't mean they should serve on my team. I realized that slightly committed, half-hearted volunteers may mean well; however, I didn't want to take the chance of ending up with an entire team of complacent, fickle volunteers. No children's ministry leader has this as a goal. Sadly, it becomes the reality when we willingly accept just anyone onto our team.

I was selective and asked questions. Why do they want to serve in children's ministry? Is it out of guilt or obligation? If so, they don't need to be on my team. Are they a good fit for your ministry? Is their heart for the children? Do they even like children? Once I determined they would be good on my team, we helped them find the best fit on the team. Many prospective volunteers would ask where the biggest need was and just wanted to be placed there. I pushed back and said, "Don't worry about my needs. Where do you feel called? In what age group do you work best?"

This was so scary, but it worked. I promise you that if you hold your standards high, remind yourself and your team that it's a privilege to serve in children's ministry, and focus on putting volunteers where they feel purpose, God will be honored by your ministry. He knows what you need. He will not let you down. Don't settle. Be selective. This will slow down that perpetual cycle.

5. Don't rush the process.

Allow your prospective volunteers the room to just be interested. Some of my best and most committed volunteers are ones who took their time, asked lots of questions, prayed, and then prayed some more before joining the team. I learned that being selective takes time and it cannot be rushed. However, the benefits are beautiful.

6. Be prepared to onboard and follow up.

My prayers were audacious, and I was expecting God to provide. We needed to be prepared for the harvest. We had onboarding supplies ready, orientation times scheduled, and trainers in place, etc.

If you are wondering if my audacious prayers worked, yes, they did! We prayed for 54 volunteers, and God gave us 55. God is in the details. He knows what we need. He called us to this position in this season. In Psalm 138:8, we are reminded that The Lord will perfect what concerns you. I challenge you to claim that promise today.

Like I mentioned before, our volunteer need is perpetual. I have done these steps many times over the past several years, and it has worked every single time. Be audacious and expect God to do it. Glitter everywhere!!!

Are you experiencing this obstacle of recruiting and retaining volunteers?

Have you or are you currently settling for "warm bodies" in your ministry?

Do you know exactly what you need? Or do you just say, "I need volunteers."?

What is your audacious prayer?

Hold My Glitter as I Tackle the Obstacle of Recruiting and Retaining Volunteers -Part 2-

Now that we have overcome the obstacle of recruiting volunteers, we need to tackle the obstacle of keeping them. In previous chapters, we talked about setting high standards, communication, etc. All of those things play a key role in retaining volunteers. In this chapter, we are going to make it a little more personal.

How do YOU feel appreciated? I know you weren't expecting that question. Do you feel appreciated when you are given a gift? Or do you feel more appreciated with words of affirmation? Maybe you are someone who feels the most appreciated when you are given help to complete a task. Or are you someone who prefers a nice hug or solid handshake? Do you feel most appreciated by the quality time that someone gives you?

My Family Pastor asked me the question, "How do YOU feel appreciated?" I knew where he was coming from because a couple of months prior to this, we were privileged to have Gary Chapman, the author of *The 5 Love Languages*, at our church for a marriage conference. (If you have never read this book, I highly recommend it.) The concept that everyone has a love language and we need to learn to speak the language of others to ensure that they feel love has fascinated me for years.

As I pondered the question that my Family Pastor asked me, my mind went straight back to something that I experienced many years ago. I had been a Children's Director at a church for a little over a year. It was Christmastime, and many of my volunteers gave me gifts and cards to show appreciation to me. I was honored by their thoughtfulness. After I opened my gifts, among all of them, I had a total of EIGHT Starbucks gift cards. You may be saying, "WHOA, that's so awesome!!!" However, to me, I was, like, "Meh, that's nice," as I placed the cards off to the side. I HATE coffee. I don't like it…not even a little.

Don't judge me. I was very grateful, and I appreciated the sentiment. I did feel love and appreciation because they thought of me. However, if they really wanted to show me love, a bottle of Diet Dr. Pepper and a card with words of affirmation would have screamed, "I LOVE AND APPRECIATE YOU." It was at this moment that I realized that my team didn't know me very well. Then I realized…I probably didn't know them well either. This made me sad.

Before I go any further, Gary Chapman's books, *The 5 Love Languages* and *The 5 Languages of Appreciation in the Workplace* have been invaluable resources for me. They are the inspiration of what I am sharing in this chapter. They have pushed me to really get to know my team better so that I am expressing appreciation and love in a way that shouts to them. I want my volunteer team to have no doubt.

As children's ministry leaders, we are always looking for ways to show appreciation to our volunteer team, as we should. My volunteer coordinator is super creative. She comes up with fun ideas to show appreciation to our volunteers. There are also websites full of ideas with clever sayings that go along with candy bars and other small items and trinkets that you can pair together to give to your team to tell them that you appreciate them and that what they do matters. This form of appreciation/gift-giving is fun and sweet and thoughtful, but is it effective? The answer is…to some yes, but not to all.

I am not saying to stop putting together fun, creative gifts for your volunteers. What I am saying is, we must be more intentional to ensure our team TRULY feels the love. If someone truly feels love and appreciation, they are inspired to keep going. They feel purpose. They feel valued. They remain serving on the team.

So how do we become more intentional in our appreciation? First and foremost, we MUST get to know our team.

Relationship

Relationship

Relationship

My friend and ministry coach, Jessica Bealer, encourages children's ministry leaders to begin with having volunteers fill out a form with questions all about them. We call ours the "All About Me" form. It has around 20 questions about their favorite things -- favorite color, favorite coffee order, favorite candy, favorite restaurants, etc. We also ask silly questions about hidden talents and how they hang the toilet paper roll (over or under). Our volunteers fill this form out as part of their onboarding process. We gain lots of personal insight about each volunteer. We can now tailor our appreciation to them.

As you get to know your volunteers, watch how they show love and appreciation to others. Most likely that is how they want it to be reciprocated. My staff and I pay very close attention to this and make a note. This information helps us show appreciate with awesomeness. The volunteer is usually blown away at the intentionality.

One of the other things I have learned from my friend, Jessica, is to have an "appreciation plan." Let's face it, ministry can get a little crazy. Unless we plan it, it's easy to fall through the cracks. Good intentions do not show love and appreciation. An appreciation plan allows you to plan some sort of appreciation each month. This plan also ensures you budget for appreciation. Examples: February you get every volunteer their favorite candy (listed on their "All About Me" form). In May you honor the volunteers who are graduating from high school. In June you honor the men of children's ministry.

When we create our appreciation plan each year, we have made sure that all love languages are represented within the plan. In February we are giving a gift. In November I will send personal handwritten thank you cards to show words of affirmation. In July we have a team picnic to have quality time with the team. In April we have a special thing we do as an act of service for our volunteers. (This is explained below.) These are just some of the examples. As you can see, no matter what love language/appreciation language speaks loudest to the volunteer, something will resonate with them throughout the year. It's not just gifts, gifts, gifts, gifts.

Two times each year we hold an appreciation/training event for our volunteers. I call it "Impact Event." The goal is for our volunteers to come together and be encouraged, trained, refreshed, resourced, loved, and appreciated. As we plan, I sit with my staff and ensure that every language of appreciation is spoken during this two-hour event.

- **Physical Touch:** They get greeted at the door with hugs and high fives.
- **Quality Time:** We seat the volunteers at round tables. There is small-group discussion time over lunch. The feedback that came back is that the volunteers LOVE this time and want it to be longer in the future.
- **Gifts:** Each volunteer is presented with a gift bag with their name on it. As a gift, we gave a devotional book and a hoodie with our children's ministry logo on it. We knew their sizes from the "All About Me" forms.
- **Acts of Service:** First of all, we hold the Impact Event during our second service on a Sunday. We get our church staff and subs to teach in our classrooms during this time so that our ENTIRE volunteer team has the

opportunity to attend. This act of honoring their time is a HUGE hit among the team. We also serve them lunch. One other way of showing acts of service is the training they received. Being resourced and set up for success is a really big deal.

- **Words of Affirmation:** We generally make a video with parents and kids sharing why they love our ministry and how they have been blessed by it. There usually is not a dry eye in the room. Another way we speak words of affirmation is to honor a few individual volunteers publicly.

Each time we do this training/appreciation it is a huge success. The team leaves fired up…all of them!

One other act of service we do each year is the "Box of Awesomeness." My staff deems this as one of their favorite things that we get to do. We create these boxes about ten days prior to Easter. First, we create a booklet with all the information and training tips we want and need to share about our upcoming Easter services. The box contains this information booklet and also contains a new children's ministry t-shirt (in their size); a new lanyard; some type of other swag, like a travel mug; and some candy. The box is then tied up nicely with a bow with the name of the volunteer on it.

Now for the fun part…delivery day. Our children's ministry staff delivers each and every box to the homes of every single volunteer in one day. We divide and conquer. We have so much fun doing it. We make it into a game and try to be "ninja-like" and not get caught putting the boxes on the porches. If we get caught, we have to take a selfie with that volunteer. Oh, and if there is a Ring camera, we always do something fun and leave some kind of message. Like I said, this appreciation activity is a favorite for us, but especially for the volunteer team. We have done this the last three years, and now they expect it and get excited. On the Sunday following delivery day, you will see them all wearing their new t-shirts as they share stories of how they found their boxes. By the way, they all actually read the Easter information booklet!

At the end of the day, the goal is to ensure that ALL of your volunteers feel loved and appreciated. No matter in which "language of appreciation" you speak to them, they will hear what you are saying. However, the way you do it will determine how loudly and confidently they hear it. Volunteers that are loved and appreciated stay serving on the team. Yep, glitter time!!!

Keeping It Real

How do you feel appreciated?

Do you know your volunteer team enough to show appreciation in a more intentional way?

What are things you have done to show volunteers they are appreciated?

What can you do to improve?

Closing

In Exodus 17:8-16, we read the story of the Amalekites coming to attack Israel. Moses told Joshua to go in and fight, and he would be on the hill raising the staff of God in his hand. When Moses held the staff up, the Israelites were overcoming. However, when Moses put his arms down and lowered the staff, the Amalekites would gain advantage. So Moses stood strong to hold his arms up until the sun set so Joshua and the army would be victorious. However, Moses soon realized he couldn't do it alone. Aaron and Hur came alongside Moses and literally helped him hold up his arms. For the duration of the battle, they stayed beside Moses to ensure victory. I like to imagine Aaron and Hur cheering Moses on. I can hear them saying, "Come on,

Moses, you've got this. You've done harder things than this. God always comes through. Don't give up, Moses! We are not giving up on you!"

What if Aaron and Hur decided not to help Moses? What if they gave up and talked Moses into putting his arms down because it was too hard? I'm so glad they didn't. This is a beautiful example of I Thessalonians 5:11 where Moses' friends served him by lifting him up. We are not meant to do life alone. God knew we would need each other. He knew that over-coming obstacles would be difficult for us. He knew when He wrote in Hebrews 10:24 for us to consider about how to encourage and love each other.

When you go into battle, who is "holding your glitter"? Who you hand off your glitter to matters. It needs to be someone who cheers you on. Your glitter-holder needs to be someone who will be honest with you and call you out when you start to lose your way and someone you will trust and will receive their counsel. In Proverbs 27:9 we are reminded that, "The heartfelt counsel of a friend is as sweet as perfume and incense" (NASB).

Find your glitter-holder and get ready to overcome your obstacles. Before long, you will begin to see your obstacles as merely opportunities to grow as a leader, and growing as a leader should be celebrated. It's a good thing you have glitter.

Meet Debbie Rhoads

If you asked Debbie how she got into children's ministry, she would tell you that she didn't go looking for it; children's ministry chose her. Debbie has been in ministry for over 30 years, 21 of those specifically dedicated to children's ministry. Throughout her time in ministry, she has served in churches of all sizes -- big, small, multi-site, and megachurch. She has held the roles of not only Children's Pastor, but also as NextGen Pastor and Leadership Development Director. Debbie is currently the Children's Ministry Director at Grace Chapel in Franklin, Tennessee.

Debbie is the author of two other books, *The Plate: The Who, What, Why, How, and How Not To's of Burnout* as well as *My Brand New Life With*

My Best Friend, Jesus. She is also a contributor to *KidzMatter Magazine*. In addition to this, Debbie is a faculty member of KidMin Academy.

Debbie holds a degree in Psychology: Christian Counseling. She is a children's counselor within her church's counseling ministry. Her heart is to help children and their families deal with the growing issues of anxiety and mental health.

Debbie and her husband reside in Franklin, Tennessee. Their two adult children also live in the Nashville area. Debbie loves to travel and experience new things, but her absolute favorite thing is being Gigi to her adorable grandson and her precious granddaughter.

Resources

Chapman, Gary D. The 5 Love Languages. Moody Publishers, 2015.

Chapman, Gary D., and Paul E. White. The 5 Languages of Appreciation in the Workplace: Empowering Organizations by Encouraging People. Northfield Publishing, 2019.

Cleveland Clinic medical. "Endorphins: What They Are and How to Boost Them." Cleveland Clinic, 2022, my.clevelandclinic.org/health/body/23040-endorphins.

Corkill, Beccy. "People Are Wondering What the Glitter Conspiracy Is All About." IFLScience, 6 July 2023, www.iflscience.com/people-are-wondering-what-the-glitter-conspiracy-is-all-about-69690.

Furtick, Steven. Sun Stand Still: What Happens When You Dare to Ask God for the Impossible. Random House, 2010.

Magazine, Outreach. "The Life Church: No. 6 Fastest-Growing Church, 2016." Outreachmagazine.Com, 6 Oct. 2016, outreachmagazine.com/ideas/19382-the-life-church.html.

Sharma, Ruchira. "Where Did Glitter Come From?" International Business Times UK, International Business Times UK, 17 Nov. 2017, www.ibtimes.co.uk/brief-history-glitter-where-it-originated-1647779.

THE PLATE

The Who, What, Why, How, and How Not To's of Burnout

by Debbie Rhoads

For more information visit kidzmatter.com